Make a Difference
in Your World

by Jaclynn Weber

ISBN: 978-0-9824098-0-0

CREDITS:
Page Layout: Linda Stubblefield
Cover Design: Julie Busby
Proofreaders: Rena Fish, Jane Grafton,
Diane Rykhus, Cindy Schaap
Photography: Alex Midence
www.photosbyalexander.net

Printed and Bound in the United States

Make a Difference in Your World

in Your World

Jaclynn
Weber

LESSONS FOR TEEN GIRLS

About the Author

JACLYNN WEBER IS the wife of Brother Todd Weber, the junior high youth pastor at First Baptist Church of Hammond, Indiana. She is the only daughter of Dr. and Mrs. Jack Schaap.

Mrs. Weber is a 2002 graduate of Hyles-Anderson College. At graduation she received the coveted "Miss Hylander" award.

Jaclynn is the author of five books which are written specifically to teenage young ladies. Mrs. Weber is an often-requested conference speaker. She serves as one of three pianists at First Baptist Church and is very involved in the music program. Jaclynn also assists her husband with the seventh grade Sunday school department and senior high teen church on Sunday mornings.

Married on June 1, 2002, the Webers are the parents of three children, Lyndsay, Raymond, and Alexys.

Dedication

I WOULD LIKE TO dedicate this book to my husband Todd and also my three children, Lyndsay, Raymond, and Alexys.

Todd,

You are the love of my life, and what a wonderful day it was when I met you. Marrying you is one of the greatest decisions I ever made. Thank you for loving me unconditionally, for taking care of me, and for loving our children. You have truly made quite a difference in my world, and I love you with all my heart.

Jaclynn

Lyndsay, Ray, and Lexy,

I want you to know that your dad and I love you. We think you are the greatest kids in the world. You are very precious to me, and you are some of the most important people in my life. I pray every day that you will grow up right and that God will give me wisdom to train you because if there is anyone's life I want to make a difference in, it is yours. I love you with all my heart.

Mom

Acknowledgments

I WOULD LIKE TO thank Linda Stubblefield for her countless hours of hard work and dedication to her job. She has been responsible for assembling each book I have written, not to mention the layout, cover design, and proofreading. She is definitely one of the hardest workers I know.

I would also like to thank Rena Fish, who has proofread each of my books, for her excellent work and attention to detail. Also, I would like to thank my mom, Cindy Schaap, Jane Grafton, and Diane Rykhus for their help with the proofreading of this book.

Thank you, Julie Busby, for your work on the cover of this book. You have such great ideas, and I appreciate your work and dedication.

A special thank you to Alex Midence for his cover photography.

Other Books
by
Jaclynn Weber

christianwomanhood.org

Table of Contents

Introduction

THE ROAD NOT TAKEN
by Robert Frost

TWO ROADS DIVERGED in a yellow wood,
And sorry I could not travel both
And be one traveler, long I stood
And looked down one as far as I could
To where it bent in the undergrowth;

Then took the other, as just as fair,
And having perhaps the better claim,
Because it was grassy and wanted wear;
Though as for that, the passing there
Had worn them really about the same,

And both that morning equally lay
In leaves no step had trodden black.

Oh, I kept the first for another day!
Yet knowing how way leads on to way,
I doubted if I should ever come back.

I shall be telling this with a sigh
Somewhere ages and ages hence:
Two roads diverged in a wood, and I—
I took the one less traveled by,
And that has made all the difference.

CHAPTER ONE

The Choice Only You Can Make

WHILE ON VACATION, I picked up a magazine, and as I was flipping through it, I saw that it was filled with Hollywood stars and the drama of their "inside" lives. The magazine contained nothing new from the same old stories we hear on the news about their crazy, mixed-up lifestyles: who broke up with whom, who overdosed on drugs, who got drunk at the last celebrity party, who had their children taken away because they (the parents, not the kids) were out of control, and on and on the list of garbage and filth goes. When I closed the magazine, I literally became sick to my stomach, but I also had several thoughts about our Christian teenage girls:

1. Why in the world would we as God's children, who are saved from that horrific lifestyle, make women and girls in Hollywood our role models?

2. The last place we should look for dating and marriage advice is from Hollywood.
3. God created and loves those people, and most of them never even acknowledge the existence of their Creator.
4. A happy marriage and a happy family are not truly depicted in the movies.
5. Prince Charming does not always show up riding on a white horse to sweep you off your feet to take you to the land of "happily ever after" at the perfect time!

There is always a new and upcoming star—just like there is always a new movie coming out for more excitement and entertainment. The lifestyles of these stars are characterized by a desire to "...*enjoy the pleasures of sin for a season.*" (Hebrews 11:25)

I am sure it would be an incredible experience to be famous and well-known by the world and have your face plastered on the television, in the movies, and in magazines; however, the corruption and filth of the lifestyle that goes along with this fame is hardly worth the pleasure, and as the Bible states in James

1:15, "...and sin, when it is finished, bringeth forth death."

I saw a famous person interviewed who is now in her sixties or early seventies, and the story of her life was extremely sad and one of loneliness. At the time of the interview, she was not making a lot of sense because of drug misuse and medications' having affected her mind. Her story was full of broken marriages, depression, doctor visits, and incredible loneliness. Her private life was not at all what she pretended to be in public.

I felt so sorry for this woman whose life had been more like a horror story than a happy life of fulfillment. She was pretending to be happy in both her public and private life, but she never figured out how to really live.

One of my many role models and heroines is my Grandma Hyles. Her life has been filled with being in the spotlight—at least in the fundamental world—and she was constantly aware of people's watching her and having to act the part of the perfect wife of one of the greatest leaders in Christianity, Dr. Jack Hyles. She

has played her part very well. Yet, she is not just graceful and poised in front of the crowd; she knows the secret to living a happy life and not just putting on a good show for everyone to admire. She finds her strength and joy not through the pleasures of sin; instead, her joy and strength come from her time alone with her God. She realizes that to please the crowds and the fans, she must first please her Saviour and accept herself the way God made her. She does not have to try to be like anyone else or please any critic; she simply has to fulfill the role God has designed for her—the role of Beverly Hyles.

What a wonderful, exciting adventure it is to go in the path that God has for us! It is the path that leads to the shining light instead of the dungeon of destruction.

To those of you who feel trapped by all of the standards and rules set for you by your parents, school, or authorities, please realize this: the greatest freedom is not found in fighting for your rights or going against the grain. The most liberating and free life is found in yielding yourself completely to God and His will and submitting to all authorities in your life.

Secondly, realize that you do not have to be like anyone else. Yes, you should have role models, but they should not be stars like Hannah Montana (Miley Cyrus). Choose some godly ladies whom you admire (yes, they can be younger) and get advice from them, but also learn that God has a path for your life that only you and He can travel. That path leads to peace, love, happiness, contentment, and freedom. All you have to do is start walking!

CHAPTER TWO

The Miracle

TEN TINY FINGERS, ten small toes,
Two little hands, a button nose,
Two perfect ears, one pretty head,
She looks so sweet inside her bed.
I watch as she drifts off to sleep,
And I think as I begin to weep—
She's a miracle.

Two other children just as dear,
I love to play and have them near.
They make me laugh (and sometimes cry),
The apples of their daddy's eye.
They're very busy—on the run,
Oh, they could go from sun to sun—
They're my miracles.

Two parents once came home with me,
They were as happy as could be.
For they had just been very scared,
And doctors had not been prepared.
Their daughter had been nearly lost,
Yet I was saved at quite a cost—
I'm their miracle.

Your parents too were once so proud
To show you off to all the crowd.
Their little one without a flaw,
You often heard them "ooh" and "aah."
They thanked the Lord for their sweet prize;
They loved your smile, endured your cries—
You are a miracle.

And too the one whose steps are slow
She does not smile; she does not know
That she is different from the rest,
Yet I think Jesus loves her best!
For He allowed her life, her birth
Though doctors could not see her worth—
She's a miracle.

Though many say to kill a child
Before she's born is very mild.
And if she has a birth defect
Though tests are not always correct,
Then let her die; why should she live?
To society, what can she give?—
She's just a miracle.

To those who dare to stand and say,
"We have our rights; we want our way;
A woman has a right to choose!"
For who has walked inside her shoes
After all, she's having fun;
Why should she pay for what she's done?
It's just a miracle.

To doctors, lawyers, women's lib,
You've sold a lie; you've told a fib.
You err in what you say and do,
It goes against the Bible true.
For God's the One Who made us all;
He chose you back before the fall—
You are a miracle.

And as I think of Heaven above
Of all those children no one loved
Looking down on earth below,
Only God will ever know
What they have missed, what they have lost
Because no one would pay the cost—
They are miracles.

So listen now and listen well,
Stay pure, stay sweet, and never sell
Your future for a night of fun.
For once it's all been said and done
You'll live with what you chose to do
And life is not a game for you—
It's a miracle.

CHAPTER THREE

The Peacemaker

A PEACEMAKER IS easy to get along with.
A peacemaker does not try to cause trouble.
A peacemaker listens more often than she talks.
A peacemaker tries to understand how others feel.
A peacemaker is unselfish and does not want her way.
A peacemaker does not blurt out what she thinks.
A peacemaker knows how to walk away.
A peacemaker solves problems with kindness.
A peacemaker lives by Proverbs 15:1 which says,
    "A soft answer turneth away wrath...."
A peacemaker asks God for wisdom and guidance.
A peacemaker does not yell and scream at anyone.
A peacemaker does not spread lies and gossip.
A peacemaker is not critical of others around her.
A peacemaker looks for the good in people.
A peacemaker is honest.

A peacemaker does not talk about people behind their backs.

A peacemaker is real.

A peacemaker walks with God.

A peacemaker respects authority.

A peacemaker looks for ways to help.

A peacemaker is a true friend.

A peacemaker loves unconditionally.

A peacemaker puts others' feelings before her own.

A peacemaker honors her parents.

A peacemaker gets along with her family.

A peacemaker does her best in school.

A peacemaker does not make false accusations.

A peacemaker does not lose her temper.

A peacemaker is not a whiner.

A peacemaker finds her joy in that which never changes.

A peacemaker is not extremely moody.

A peacemaker brings joy to those around her.

A peacemaker does not complain.

A peacemaker tries to make her world a better place.

A peacemaker does not listen to negative talk.

A peacemaker believes one is innocent until proven guilty.

A peacemaker finds strength and wisdom through God's Word.

A peacemaker loves everyone.

A peacemaker does not think about herself.

A peacemaker does not look down on anyone.

A peacemaker cares for those less fortunate than she.

A peacemaker loves to laugh.

A peacemaker cries with the one who is hurting.

A peacemaker does not rejoice in another's misfortune.

A peacemaker never seeks revenge.

A peacemaker is appropriate in every situation.

A peacemaker is not loud and stubborn.

A peacemaker seeks to please God and her parents first.

Matthew 5:9 says, *"Blessed are the peacemakers: for they shall be called the children of God."* Are you a peacemaker?

CHAPTER FOUR

God Is My Refuge

WHAT DO YOU do when your world falls apart? Where do you go for help?

- To whom would you run if your mother walked out on you?
- How would you make it if your dad was too busy for you?
- Where would you run if your mother was so drunk she did not know who you were and where she was?
- How do you know that God will be there for you if those who are closest to you abandon you?
- How would you deal with a mother who was constantly unfaithful to your father?
- Who sees you if you cut yourself and take those "uppers" or "downers" to help you handle your

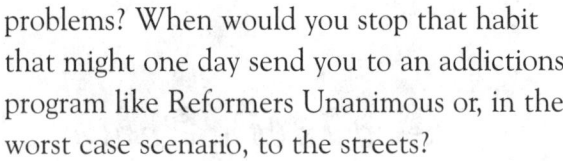

problems? When would you stop that habit that might one day send you to an addictions program like Reformers Unanimous or, in the worst case scenario, to the streets?

- Who sees your grief over the loss of a beloved sister as you silently stand and watch her casket lowered into the ground, never to be seen on this earth again?

- To whom can you tell your deepest thoughts and know you can trust Him?

You probably already know to Whom I am referring, but have you found Him?

Life is full of worst-case scenarios that happen when we least expect them, and the ones I have listed at the beginning of this article are just a drop of water in the floods that we have experienced in our youth group and church. Sometimes I hurt so much for our teenagers when I think of some of the seemingly horrible things that they face, and I say in my heart, "How are they ever going to make it?" Of course there is an answer, but I wonder sometimes if they will find it.

This chapter was written with a particular girl in mind to give her some encouragement, but I know that our church and youth group are not the only ones with problems, and I hope these next few words will be a help to those of you who feel that you are all alone and have nowhere to turn.

I want to tell you that first of all, I wish you did not have to go through this heartache all by yourself, but then again, with God, you are never completely alone. I used to look at the lives of the kids on our bus route (and now in teen church), and as some of them would lash out with cruel words or make a scene to get attention, I would feel so sorry for them. They are frustrated and hurt because, at such a young age, they have already been used and abused by the world. They have not been taught respect and common decency, but instead have been beaten, sworn at, yelled at, thrown around, and neglected by those who are supposed to take care of them. It is a miracle that any of them survive and have a halfway decent life.

I say this because I know some of you have many problems in your life, but you are not alone in your

hurt. Many others are desperate for love and for someone to care, and they need you. If you understand what it is like to feel lonely and abandoned, you may be just the one who can give them the love and encouragement they need. God never has someone suffer for no reason. He says in Romans 8:28, "...*all things work together for good to them that love God, to them who are the called according to his purpose*," and there is much good that will come out of your pain—though you may not be able to see that yet. You may not see it for many months or even years, but it will come. God does not break His promises.

Secondly, everyone—no matter how strong or seemingly problem-free—needs God. I will say this in a million different ways until I am convinced beyond a doubt that you believe it: you need God! Only He can get you through your situation. The difference between the life of Dr. Jack Schaap, our pastor, and the man who sits in prison today waiting for execution is God and God alone. It is with His help that we either accept the life we have been given with gratitude and humility or become bitter and filled with

contempt and hatred against God and all that is good. There is no other choice: God or Satan, Heaven or Hell, good or bad, right or wrong, and the decision is a simple one that people often complicate.

If you choose God, you automatically choose right, Heaven, and good. No, life will not always be easy, but it will be a wonderful life, and you will never regret it. However, if you choose Satan, you choose wrong, bad, and Hell, and your life will be filled with remorse and regrets. You may have some good times, but overall, it will be a sad and wasted life. I beg you to choose wisely, not as others in your life may have chosen, but as those whom you admire and respect have chosen. You will never regret making the right decision.

Lastly, I want to tell you that no matter how rotten your life seems or how much pain you have gone through, it is not an excuse for you to fail, nor does it give you permission to do anything you want to do. You have a choice to make. You can go out in the world and throw away everything you have been taught at church and say, "It did not work for my family, so it won't work for me." You could also deny that your family has any problems and live just like them, or you can choose to serve God no matter what anyone else does. I wish I could say that if you choose to serve God, you will have a life of ease and comfort. You may have a comparatively easy life, but I cannot say that for sure. I only know that true joy, happiness, and contentment are found through following God and doing His will—whatever that may be.

I am here for you. Your pastor and youth pastor are there for you. Many people in your church would give you the shirt off their back if they knew you needed it. God is always there for you. He is your refuge.

Have you ever been afraid of something that you could not control? When we had tornados come through our area last year, I remember sitting outside on the porch with my husband and watching the storm and alternately thinking, "God is really powerful," and "I hope a tornado doesn't hit our house!" I was scared, and there was not anything I could humanly do to stop those tornados. We eventually went inside because it got too windy to stay outside. Our house became our refuge that night. We went in

to stay safe and dry and away from the 80+ miles per hour winds that could have picked us up right off our feet! I was very thankful for a place I could run to and hide from that dangerous storm.

Well, God can be that refuge for you right now. If you run to Him, He can hide you from the danger that is around you, and He can protect you from your pain and hurt. God is there all the time, shielding you from the storms of life.

Let Him protect you, let your leaders guide you, and let the mistakes of others be a lesson to you not to choose the way they have gone. I love you, and I believe in you, but never forget that no one loves you like God does.

CHAPTER FIVE

The Heart of God

I KNOW YOUR LIVES are busy with school work, youth activities, summer camp, chores, or part-time jobs. No doubt you are often busy with homework, term papers, class projects, and all the extras. Those of you who are seniors will try to squeeze all you can out of the last few months of school and count down the days to graduation. Junior highers will be busy with science fairs, band classes, sports, and trying to pass algebra. Those of you turning 16 are probably trying to get your driver's license and a car (or access to a car) as quickly as possible.

I know you are extremely busy, and it's all good. You have little time for anything else—good or bad— but I just wondered if you would mind taking a minute to read something I wrote for you. It's kind of long, and I know you cannot read it all in one day, but maybe you could read just a few words sometime during your hectic, crazy schedule.

I was hoping maybe, just maybe, you would be able to squeeze it in somewhere before you lie down exhausted at the end of the day. It's not that I need you to read it to make Me happy; it's just that I have so much to tell you in this Letter I've written to you. I wish you could visit Me in person and listen to everything I have to say. But since a personal visit is not a part of the plan right now, My Letter will have to do.

I wish you could call Me on the phone and hear Me tell you what is on My mind and in My heart. I wish you could understand My love for you and the dreams and goals I hope to see fulfilled. I wish all of your tears could be wiped away and all of your pain erased. I wish you could share with Me the exciting moments in your life and all of the great times you have. I just wish you could possibly know how much I care about you, but I fear you never will.

Sometimes I wonder if you will ever know the depth of love I have for you—a love so strong it cost

My life, and yet it often does not seem to be enough, for you still are so distant from Me.

I wonder if you will ever know the joy I have when I see you happy and the grief and pain I feel in your loss. So often you are not aware of Me, yet I am always there for you.

When you rejoice, the heavens ring with laughter, and when you cry, all Heaven weeps. I love to see you smile, and it hurts to see your tears.

I know how it feels to be lonely for I was lonely too. I know what it's like to be mocked and scorned for I also experienced shame.

I understand the hurt of being falsely accused and treated unfairly for that has happened to Me. In fact, I have felt every pain and hurt you are going through for I was once your age also.

I have felt the deepest sorrow and suffered the ultimate pain, yet the pain I endured when I was on earth cannot begin to compare with the hurt and rejection I feel from those whom I love the most.

Yet I knew that this would happen and that my love would be taken for granted. That is why I wrote you a Letter. I wanted to tell you so many things, but I knew often you would be too busy to care. My greatest desire is that those whom I love would know Me and feel the love I have for them.

So whenever you get an opportunity, I hope you will take the time to read My Letter to you. I do not care when or where you read it or how much you read. I just want you to begin to see how much I love you. I want you to let Me help you with your problems and your hurts, and I want you to spend time with Me.

I have been waiting for so long to comfort and guide you, yet I have never been asked. I have so much wisdom and advice to give, yet it has never been sought. I can see the end of the road you travel as I watch you stagger blindly on your own. I know the answer to every question you have, but you do not seek My knowledge.

And so today, just another ordinary day that I created, I ask you again: Will you read My letter? Will you let Me help you through your problems? Will you ask Me for wisdom and strength? I am here, ready to give you anything you need. I have always been here since the day you prayed and asked Me to come into your heart.

CHAPTER SIX

Whatsoever Thy Hand Findeth to Do...

I LOVE VACATIONS! WE just went to Montana and Canada and had the best time! Next week we are going to visit my grandparents in Michigan, and I am looking forward to seeing them.

I love to sleep in! One of my favorite things to do on vacation is sleep in! It's so nice to wake up bright and early—at the crack of noon! However, I do not get to sleep in very often, so I think that is why I enjoy it so much when I do get some extra sleep.

I love lazy summer days when I get to relax, swim, or do whatever I want. I love to read, be outside, play tennis, take walks, ride bikes, or just lie around! I sound like quite the couch potato, don't I?

But do you know what I enjoy even more than

vacations, sleeping in, and time off? I love to work! It's a good thing too because most of the year I am not on vacation, and most days I begin teaching piano lessons early in the morning, and there are not many days where I get to lie around and do "nothing" (unless I am ill). Thankfully, I have two hardworking parents who taught me that work is fun, and I have a husband who is one of the hardest workers I know.

God's Word has much to say about the importance of work and doing a job well:

Ecclesiastes 9:10a, *"Whatsoever thy hand findeth to do, do it with thy might."*

II Thessalonians 3:10, *"…that if any would not work, neither should he eat."*

Proverbs 31:13, *"She [the virtuous woman] seeketh wool, and flax, and worketh willingly with her hands."*

Proverbs 6:6, *"Go to the ant, thou sluggard; consider her ways, and be wise."* (Read Proverbs 6:6-19.)

My dad has often said that God uses liars, cheaters, murderers, fornicators, and all kinds of sinful people, but He does not use lazy people. You have probably heard these sayings through the years:

- "The harder I work, the luckier I get."
- "Proper preparation prevents poor performance."
- "Greatness is not in the performance; it's in the preparation."
- "Practice makes perfect."

My Grandpa Schaap is a successful businessman who lives a comfortable retired life and can afford pretty much anything he wants. His life has not always been this easy though. When he and my grandmother were first married, they were very poor and could not afford to live on their own. Several years later when my dad was a little boy, my grandfather decided to start a mobile home business. For many years it was very long hours with very little pay, and often it seemed like a struggle to survive. However, after many years of hard work, sweat, and toil, he became very successful. He did not "strike it rich" because he won the lottery or had a rich uncle pass away. He simply worked hard, and God blessed him.

I enjoyed school, especially the social part, but I

do not miss all of the reports, exams, tests, quizzes, and finals that seemed always to be looming ahead. Yet, looking back, I can see that those were simply tools to teach me how to work and prepare for the more difficult tests and quizzes life would bring to me.

My parents were extremely picky where I worked as a teenager, but they did encourage me to work. As a little girl, I had my list of chores I had to do every day, and in junior high I had babysitting jobs and worked odd jobs here and there. At 15, I began teaching piano lessons and am still teaching them.

As a wife, mother, and piano teacher, as well as having many other things I do, my life is filled with work. If I had not learned to enjoy work and to make it fun, then I would have a pretty rotten life. Vacations come once or twice a year, but my work goes on day after day. Days off from being a wife and a mother are nonexistent, and there are no such things as "personal and sick days" to stop life from happening.

So my point is this: girls, you need to learn how to work! If you do not enjoy working, you had better learn to love it fast! Did you know girls can mow, rake, pull weeds, paint, wash cars, shovel dirt, take out the trash, buy groceries, clean the garage, and shovel snow as well as do dishes, babysit, bake, dust the furniture, and do laundry? Just because we are girls does not mean we cannot get our hands dirty. The virtuous woman worked willingly with her hands, and the Bible even talks about her helping with the garden and the crops. She was a woman, but I do not believe she was a "priss."

It is important to read your Bible, pray, and go soul winning, but one of the most spiritual things you can do is work hard and learn to do your very best at every job you are given to do. If you learn, like Mary Poppins did, to make your job fun, then you will have a happy, wonderful life, and "every task you undertake becomes a piece of cake" and "in every job that must be done there is an element of fun!" In my opinion, you will love life if you learn to love work!

CHAPTER SEVEN

I Have a Dream

"I HAVE A DREAM…" were famous words spoken by Dr. Martin Luther King, Jr. as he spoke against the unfair treatment of African-Americans in our nation. He had a dream that our country would treat black people and white people equally.

Walt Disney had a dream that began as a young boy to create a place, "a magical world" where families could get away from their jobs and the pressures of life and enjoy spending time together. His dream became a reality when Disneyland opened its park for the first time.

Everyone has dreams.

- My father had a dream of going into business with his dad. He gave up his dream to become a preacher.
- My husband had a dream of being a basketball

star after high school, but he changed his dreams when God called him to go to Bible college and work with teenagers.

- I had a dream as a four-year-old girl of being a missionary to Haiti, the poorest country in the western hemisphere.

My dreams changed drastically by age 15. As a sophomore in high school, I wanted to graduate; buy a red Mustang convertible with a V-8 engine, a tan top, and a tan-leather interior; live in a condo in downtown Chicago; and be a single businesswoman for a large corporation. Obviously, my dreams have changed!

I went to Hyles-Anderson College (the greatest Bible college in the world!), met and married Todd Weber, and my life is happier than my own dreams could have ever made me.

It is important to have dreams and goals for your life, and I do not think it is possible to dream too much or too big.

Whenever I ask the girls in my Sunday school class what they dream for their life, I often receive one of

two answers: to be a teacher or to be a singer. Those are not bad dreams, and I would rather someone have lots of dreams and lots of goals than to have none at all. There is nothing worse than a teenager whose biggest, most exciting goal in life is to flip hamburgers and play X-Box for the rest of his boring days.

As you dream and as you make goals for yourself, remember that God created you with a specific purpose in mind. The dreams you have for yourself are rather miniscule compared to the future that awaits you in the will of God.

We think we know what we are good at, and we think we know what we want, but do you know what? We don't have a clue! How could we know ourselves better than the God Who created us, Who formed our minds and personalities, and Who knows everything about us, including all our quirks?

My dad has often told about the visiting preacher who came up to him when he was a teenager and asked him if he had ever prayed about God's will for his life. He asked my dad to pray about it, so my dad did. He prayed a very simple prayer: "Dear God, the

preacher asked me to pray about Your will, so I am. Amen."

A few months later another man of God asked my dad the same question, and Dad prayed a similar prayer. Yet, it was still several months before God spoke to his heart and called him to preach. You see, Dad had good dreams—big dreams—for his life, but they were not God's dreams for him, and he knew it.

Maybe some of you are struggling with a dream in your life that, deep inside, you know is not what God has for you. Maybe you are afraid, like I was for a while, that God's dreams are not going to be as thrilling or glamorous as the dreams you have for yourself.

Let me say from experience and on behalf of everyone who has given up dreams and exchanged them for God's perfect plan, nothing in the world will make you happier, more fulfilled, and more content, and no career out there is as important and as exciting as the purpose God has for you.

God's will is more thrilling than the wildest ride at Cedar Point, more adventurous than an African safari, more glamorous than the life that any Hollywood star could ever experience. And the best part is, you are the only one in the world who can do it.

So, dream big, but in the end, let God have His way. You will never regret it!

CHAPTER EIGHT

Thy God Is My God

RUTH 1:16 SAYS, "AND *Ruth said, Intreat me not to leave thee, or to return from following after thee: for whither thou goest, I will go; and where thou lodgest, I will lodge: thy people shall be my people, and thy God my God.*"

At this writing our Hammond Baptist High School graduation was just a few weeks ago, and already I have noticed that some graduates seem to be throwing away everything they have been taught in order to do their own thing. Most of our graduates are planning to attend Hyles-Anderson College or another Bible college, and most of them are planning to serve God with their lives. Yet there are always a few who don't seem to "catch" what has been instilled in them since they were young and reinforced throughout their 18 years of attending church and a Christian school.

I began going to church when I was two weeks old. My mom put me in the nursery, and church became a big part of my life long before I could even talk! I was taught at church, as well as at home, about Jesus, the Bible, and Heaven when I could not even say my ABC's. Then, at the age of five, I began going to our Christian school, and the Bible stories and songs and their truths were ingrained in me over and over again every day.

I went to a Christian school from K-5 through twelfth grade and then on to Hyles-Anderson College (which I believe to be the greatest Bible college in the world!), and there I was taught still more about God's Word and the Christian life. So for the first 21 years of my life, God's Word and the Christian life were taught over and over and over again to me.

Reading about my life may cause some to think I never had to decide to serve God, and it might seem like all of my decisions about serving God, having standards, and living right were already made for me, and just like a Christian robot, I followed the path that was already put before me.

In Ruth chapter one in the Bible, Ruth had a decision to make. She could either stay in her home country with her family and friends or go with her mother-in-law to live in a strange country where she knew no one. Ruth felt like she should go with her mother-in-law, and in choosing to go, she chose her lifestyle, her Christianity, her standards and convictions, and her God.

Like Ruth, I had to choose which path I would take. No matter how much preaching and teaching were "pounded" into my head from a young age, a point still came in my life where I had to decide for myself what road I would take. Would I follow the path that had been laid out before me, or would I choose another path that would lead to a very different end?

The current graduates are no different from many with whom I graduated in 1999. Although the same Bible and the same standards had been taught to them, they truly did not get it. Yes, they may know a lot about God in their head, but they do not have His Word in their heart. Their mind tells them God is

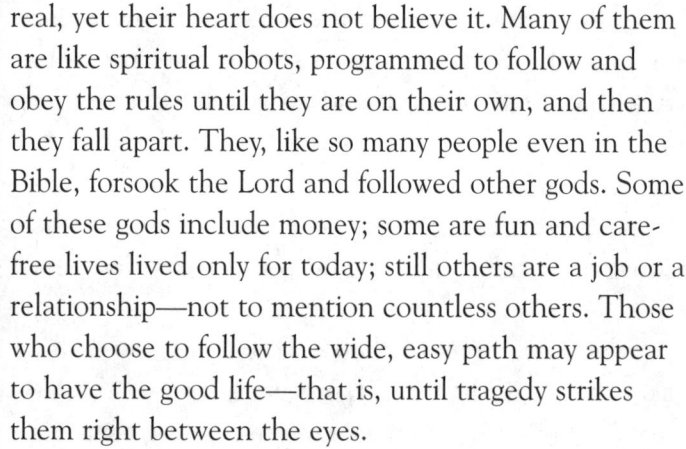

real, yet their heart does not believe it. Many of them are like spiritual robots, programmed to follow and obey the rules until they are on their own, and then they fall apart. They, like so many people even in the Bible, forsook the Lord and followed other gods. Some of these gods include money; some are fun and care-free lives lived only for today; still others are a job or a relationship—not to mention countless others. Those who choose to follow the wide, easy path may appear to have the good life—that is, until tragedy strikes them right between the eyes.

Statistics show that one out of every two marriages (including Christians') end in divorce, that one out of four women will develop cancer, and that nearly one out of two women will lose a child through miscarriage. I am not trying to sound morbid; I'm just saying that life is not always easy, and going through it without God is miserable and depressing.

We all think we are fine until something bad happens; then to Whom do we cry out in our heartache? God! What do we do in desperation? We cry out for God to help us. How selfish it is to think we can

ignore God and live our own lives and then run to His side during a trial.

Why do we have dress standards? Why do we read our Bible and pray? Why is it so important to go to church and to get to know God? These are questions you must learn to answer, and the correct answer is not "because we have to."

When it comes time for you to decide which path to follow, will you choose the one that has been set before you? Life is good, but it is not always easy, and when the hard times come, I want to have God on my side! Do you?

CHAPTER NINE

One Nation—Under God

"I PLEDGE ALLEGIANCE TO the flag of the United States of America, and to the Republic for which it stands, one Nation under God, indivisible, with liberty and justice for all."

I have stood with my hand over my heart hundreds of times throughout my school years and recited the famous "Pledge of Allegiance" to our flag. I am thankful to live in a free country, and I am grateful to those who have sacrificed and are sacrificing even today so I can have freedom.

We live in a mighty nation—a powerful country that has been built by great leaders—leaders who through sweat, toil, and sometimes even war led our land to greatness. These men believed in their cause, and they stood for truth and right. But it is not they alone who have made our nation great, for they also

believed that under God our country would prosper. The great men in history who have helped to shape our nation knew that alone they were powerless, but with God they could do anything.

Sadly, many of our leaders today have forgotten those two small words—under God—and have done everything in their power to remove Him from our land. They are blinded by Satan's lies that man alone can do anything and does not need God, and our country has been deeply wounded and weakened because of some of their foolish decisions. God tells us in the Bible that if we do not serve Him and follow in His ways that He will punish us. Although He is a God of compassion and mercy, eventually His mercy does run out when we fail to ask forgiveness and turn to Him.

God created us, and it hurts Him deeply when we do not want anything to do with Him. Imagine how a mother and a father would feel when their son or daughter breaks their heart. The child whom they loved and cared for year after year and trained to serve God suddenly decides he no longer needs his parents.

He feels that he is wise enough to make his own decisions and foolishly walks out on them, not realizing that he is killing them on the inside.

God's love cannot even be compared to a parent's love because He loves us immeasurably and unfailingly. Yet we seem like we do not need Him, and we treat Him like a stranger we cannot trust. We put more confidence and trust in ungodly people like rock stars and movie idols than the God Who created them.

I believe with all of my heart that God hears the prayers of teenagers just as much as God hears the prayers of great men of faith who lead our nation and churches today. I believe God put you not only in the greatest country in the world, but also in a Christian home and church for a reason. He wanted you to live here, and He knew you would get saved and know God as a young person.

So, let me ask you this: what are you going to do with the incredible opportunities God has given you? Are you simply enjoying the luxuries of living in the richest country in the world, enjoying the latest technology (DVDs, I-Pods, Blue-Tooth, cell phones,

Internet, X-Box, etc., etc., etc.), pouring over the latest movie release, or do you comprehend the great responsibility you have been given?

As citizens of the United States of America, we have a duty to our country just as much as the soldier fighting in Iraq; and as a child of the King of kings, we owe Him our life, for it is in Him that we have every breath to breathe. Even the atheist who blasphemes His holy name breathes His air as he curses our Lord and Saviour.

So let me ask you: what are you doing for our nation? Allow me to share with you several ways you can be a part of helping our country turn back to God.

1. **Pray for our country every day.** Pray for our President and our leaders to have the wisdom they need to make the right decisions.
2. **Be a soul winner.** Learn to be soul conscious. It is good to have a set time to go soul winning, but learn to win people to the Lord at times other than your "soul-winning time."
3. **Pass out tracts.** Keep tracts in your purse and

pass them out wherever you go. Be aware that people everywhere need to hear about God.

4. **Stand up for right in your school.** Whether you are in a Christian school or public school, you must still stand for right. Don't let the "cool" crowd be the right crowd. They, and not those who love God, should feel like the misfits.

5. **Do your best to have a good relationship with the authorities in your life.** There will always be some people who are harder to get along with than others, yet every authority in your life has been placed there by God, so you should do your best to respect and obey them.

In closing, let me say that I do believe there is something each of us can do to help our country to stay free and turn back to God. Do you believe that? What are you doing to help your nation, and how are you showing your Creator and Saviour that you love Him?

Remember, we are one nation under God, and without Him, we cease to exist. Let's do what we can to make a difference in our land and for our Lord.

CHAPTER TEN

Jealousy—A Raging Fire

I HAD A FRIEND in school who was gorgeous. She was tall, blonde, and beautiful, and sometimes when I was with her, I felt very much like a short, plain brunette. Often when we would be walking somewhere, it would seem like everyone (at least the teenage guys) would immediately notice her, and I would feel invisible.

She was my best friend, and we grew up together; yet, as close as we were, at times I felt inferior and, yes, even jealous of her natural grace (as I tripped over books and sometimes my own two feet) and her beauty. It took me many years before I learned to accept the fact that I would never be "tall, blonde, and strikingly beautiful" and that God had created me just the exact way He wanted me to look.

Sometimes jealousy is good. In II Corinthians 11:2,

Paul tells the people, *"For I am jealous over you with godly jealousy...."* Even God says He is jealous in Exodus 34:14, which says, *"For thou shalt worship no other god: for the LORD, whose name is Jealous, is a jealous God."* However, most of our jealousy is the wrong kind. I would like to tell you that my jealousy has always been the godly kind, but if I told you that, I would be lying.

Jealousy comes when we do not accept how God has made us or the situation in which God has placed us. Often people become jealous when someone is chosen for an honor or a position, and those who do not get it think inwardly they were the best choice, and they do not understand why no one else chose them.

- A girl is chosen for tournament queen, and the other girls feel like they should have won.
- A girl dates a guy only to find out he is really interested in her best friend.
- Someone else at school or church is the height you would like to be or has the beautiful, long hair you wish you had. You are angry because

God gave you short, thin hair that takes years to grow an inch.

These may seem like little things, but all of them can become "giant green monsters" of jealousy if we let them. The Bible says in Proverbs 6:34a, *"For jealousy is the rage of a man,"* and in Song of Solomon 8:6 the Bible says that it is *"...cruel as the grave...."* It is like a fire that is started, and if you do not put it out right away, it will get way out of control. Jealousy is a common sin because it is in our nature not to accept ourselves as God has made us.

If you are a preacher's kid (P.K.), there will always be people who are jealous of your name or the fact that they are not a P.K., and in their minds, every honor or position a P.K. receives is only because of his/her name. You will have to deal with that attitude like I have had to at times.

Still, we must learn to accept the way God made us, the family He put us in, the color of hair and eyes He gave us, and the personality we have because of Him. (Notice we do not have control over any of these areas—God chose them all.)

Psalm 139:14, which is my favorite verse in the whole Bible, says, *"I will praise thee; for I am fearfully and wonderfully made: marvellous are thy works; and that my soul knoweth right well."* God created me perfectly in His eyes, and that knowledge gives me confidence. He decided in what family I should be, and that gives me security. He has a plan for my life, and that knowledge gives me joy.

I accept the life God has given me, the way He has made me (even my wide feet!), and the family in which He has placed me, and I refuse to let jealousy burn within me like a raging fire. I challenge you to do the same.

CHAPTER ELEVEN

Initiative—Just Do It!

I TAUGHT THE FOLLOWING formula for initiative, or you could call it a formula for success, to my eleventh grade girls in Sunday school recently. Dr. Wendell Evans, the president emeritus of Hyles-Anderson College, taught it to me in one of his classes, and I have used this formula over and over again.

1. Set a goal.
2. Plan your work.
3. Work your plan.
4. Don't get sidetracked.

If you follow these four steps, you will be successful in every area of your life, and you will also have the initiative needed to do great things for God. Now, let's discuss these steps in this chapter.

Set a Goal.

Have goals in your life that you would like to reach. Have dreams for yourself. Yes, it is important to do what God has for you, but it is not wrong to have dreams and hopes and plans for your future. Where do you want to be five or ten years from now? Do you see yourself happily married or in a Christian college or serving God someplace? Do you see yourself doing anything? Set a goal or several goals for yourself, like staying pure to the wedding altar or dating only someone whom you would consider marrying.

It is also smart to set short-term goals for yourself. Maybe you need to lose a few pounds, or maybe you need to save up some money to buy your parents something for Christmas. Set small goals for yourself, within your reach, that you can achieve. You will feel better about yourself when you reach them.

Plan Your Work.

Figure out a step-by-step way to reach your goal. For instance, if you have a goal to date only guys whom you would consider marrying, then decide who those guys would be (in your school or whom you know—of course, you can't decide now if you don't know them), ask your parents or pastor before saying yes to anyone, and have a planned "no" answer for those whom you would not consider. You do not have to be a snob or rude to others to be a good Christian! Be kind and thoughtful, but plan out how you will turn down the wrong kind of guy if he asks you out.

If you decide to lose weight, plan how you are going to do it. Maybe you are going to stop drinking pop; maybe you are not going to eat dessert or chocolate for a week; maybe you are going to exercise three times a week. Whatever it is, plan how you are going to reach your goal.

Work Your Plan.

This is the hard part because this is where character comes in. You set a goal, you planned how to reach it, and now you have to find a way to get it done. If your goal is losing weight, maybe you planned to get up early and go jogging or run on a treadmill. I guarantee you the first time your alarm goes off in the morning, you will not feel like "working your plan"!

I traveled on tour for our college one summer, and we went with Rocco and Jennifer Dapice and their six-month-old son R.J. Mrs. Dapice loved to jog, and she asked us one day if we would like to go with her at 5:00 in the morning. Well, we did not want to gain weight on tour, so we thought this was a good idea—until 5:00 a.m. rolled around!

The first morning we helped each other get up and fumbled around for our shoes and clothes in the dark since not everyone was going. Three of us finally stumbled out the door still half asleep and wishing we were still in bed. We saw the sun rise that morning, and there is nothing more beautiful than watching the sun rise over the majestic mountains out West (of course, I'd rather watch it from my warm bed), and we made it through our first hour of jogging.

Day after day, we dragged ourselves out of bed to jog with faithful, dedicated Mrs. Dapice; and day after day, we wished we were still warm and snug under our covers. It was definitely hard work jogging every morning at 5:00 a.m., but when we finished tour and still weighed the same and felt more in shape than ever, we felt like we had accomplished something, and we learned character from Mrs. Dapice's practically pushing us out of bed sometimes!

Don't Get Sidetracked.

Satan is a master at sidetracking us and getting us off of the right track. Don't let him keep you from reaching your goals. Don't let him use a handsome, "too-good-to-be-true" guy to keep you from staying pure. Don't get in a situation where you are alone with a guy—any guy—if you have made it your goal to stay pure. If your goal is to marry a preacher, don't date someone whose goal is to be a lawyer. If your goal is to make a lot of money (which is not a great goal to have), then don't date a guy who is going into the ministry because you will never be content, and he will never feel like he can please you.

So, set your goal, plan your work, work your plan, and don't get sidetracked. With God's help and this plan, your life will be a fulfilling, successful story with no regrets.

CHAPTER TWELVE

Be a Loner

IF YOU WANT TO disobey your parents, do it alone.

If you want to live your own life, do it alone.

If you don't want to listen to your pastor, do it alone.

If you want to ruin your lungs with smoking, do it alone.

If you want to listen to rock music, do it alone.

If you want to date the wrong guy, do it alone.

If you want to dress like a man, do it alone.

If you want to destroy your liver with alcohol, do it alone.

If you decide to sneak off to the movies, do it alone.

If you cheat on a test, do it alone.

If you lie to your youth director, do it alone.

If you watch worldly movies, do it alone.

If you are looking at things on the Internet you have no business looking at, do it alone.

If you want to ruin your life, do it alone.

If you spend time with God, you will have
   to do it alone.

If you want to listen to your parents, you will have
   to do it alone.

If you decide to dress right, you will have
   to do it alone.

If you listen to the right kind of music, you will have
   to do it alone.

If you decide to make church a priority, you will have
   to do it alone.

If you obey your youth pastor, you will have
   to do it alone.

If you choose the right friends, sometimes you will
   have to stand alone.

If you decide to keep your body pure, you will have
   to do it alone.

If you decide to be honest, you will have
   to do it alone.

If you decide to talk right, you will have to do it alone.

If you decide to listen to your authorities, you will
   have to do it alone.

If you decide to live a life worth living, you will have to do it alone.

You see, teenager, your friends will not always be around to encourage you to do right or wrong. Many times, no matter what decisions you make, you will be all alone.

At the end of the drinking party when you recover from your hangover, you will eventually be left all alone to think about the stupid mistake you made by going to that so-called "fun" party. When you wake up the next morning with the realization that you lost your most prized possession, your purity, you will be all alone with your guilt and regret, and when you learn you are going to have a baby, don't expect the father to be there. No, you will bring that child into the world and rear him all alone.

On the other hand, when you decide to resist the temptation of going to the party where you know there will be drinking, you will have to do it alone. You will wake up the next morning alone, without a hangover but with a guilt-free conscience. When you say "no" to that guy who cannot seem to keep his hands off of you, you will be alone, but you will have no regrets.

At some point in your life, you will have to learn to stand alone. God gives each of us a free will to make our own decisions. A wise teenager uses authorities in his life to make his decisions. A foolish teenager makes decisions on his own, and the sad thing is, it affects not only him, but many others around him also.

If you decide to do wrong and mess up your life, that is your own foolish decision. But at least have the decency not to bring others down in the gutter with you. Before you decide how you want to live your life, think of that younger sister who looks up to you and adores you; remember that girl in your youth group who wants to be just like you when she's your age. You may make a wrong decision on your own, but you will always bring someone down with you.

Friends leave, boyfriends betray you, sometimes pastors and parents let you down or even pass away. How do you want to feel about the decisions you made when it is just you and God—alone? Before you make decisions based on what is popular now, just remember that after you are old and gray and have gone to Heaven, you will stand before God—alone.

CHAPTER THIRTEEN

God Will Listen to Our Call

SOMETIMES I WONDER if God sees
The creation He has wrought
The ones through sacrifice and pain
And His own blood He bought.

I wonder if He looks at us
Through disappointed eyes,
And as He looks would shed a tear
And ask His Father, "Why?"

I wonder if He feels alone,
So untouched by us all.
Just hoping that someone would speak,
And on His name would call.

Our lives began so we could praise
Creator, Saviour, Lord.

He wanted us to talk to Him,
And love His Holy Word.

It's sad how far we've gone astray
From what He chose for us.
He chose for us true holiness;
We've chosen greed and lust.

We've chosen now to mock the One
Who gives us air to breathe.
We've ruined and destroyed our lives;
Yes, we have been deceived.

Our eyes have turned from Jesus Christ
To money, power, fame.
We're so busy with our jobs,
We've put His Word to shame.

We chase the glamorous, the new,
Run over sick and old,
We want the biggest and the best—
No matter what is sold.

We idolize the movie stars
The music singers too.
We treat them with such dignity
No matter what they do.

They shave their head, so we shave ours.
No matter how we look,
We do not even care to ask
What God says in His Book.

We starve ourselves 'cause they all do.
And that makes it okay?
We focus so much on ourselves,
More each passing day.

We try to blend in with the crowd,
And who wants to stand out?
For if you try to take a stand
You're lied and talked about.

And don't say Jesus' name too loud,
Or else someone will hear!

The atheist will tear you down;
Our government will sneer.

Even in our Christian schools,
God is not very "cool."
If you do right and take a stand,
You will be called a fool.

It's time for us to take a stand
Against unrighteousness.
To be a witness for our Lord,
His Holy Name to bless.

I challenge you to fight for right
In school, and church, and home.
Now be aware—I warn you now,
At times you'll feel alone.

Pray for God to send us now
Revival in our schools,
Put down the wrong, increase the right,
God's mercy now to rule.

Pray for the man God has for you,
That God would keep him pure,
Pray Satan will not get his mind
That he would not allure.

Then you prepare yourself for him,
As much as you now can.
Seek God's face and read His Word.
Ask God to bless "your man."

We need some girls who aren't afraid
To stand up for the Lord.
To let the Devil have his way
We simply can't afford.

I beg of you to join with me
And fight for truth and right.
Fight on your knees and on your face
Pleading for God's might.

If ever we need Christian girls
Who aren't ashamed to stand,

We need you now—yes, all of you.
Pray for our hurting land.

And I believe if we will pray,
Together, you and I
That God will listen to our call
And save us from on High.

Yes, I believe that God will hear;
Revival we will see
For God is great and merciful,
And He loves you and me.

CHAPTER FOURTEEN

I Don't Want to Die!

A HIGH SCHOOL STUDENT was having a hard time fitting into her new school. She felt alone and isolated from the crowd, and she was not making friends very easily. Day after lonely day and night after long night, she would go home, do her homework, and cry herself to sleep—only to get up the next day and do the same thing again.

One particular day had been especially hard, and as she walked home from school, she truly felt invisible. No friends, no dating life, not even any close acquaintances—life was starting to seem pointless to her. "Why does it matter that I am here anyway?" she asked herself. "No one even knows that I am alive. It wouldn't even matter if I were dead." She began convincing herself that life was not worth living.

She decided then and there that it would be better

for her to end it all and be put out of her misery than to continue living another day. When she got home, she would get the gun out of her dad's drawer, go into her room, lock the door, and end it all.

She began to pick up the pace in anxious anticipation about what she was going to do. No sooner had she reached the front door of their ranch-style house and dropped her bookbag to the floor when the phone began to ring. "It's probably Mom calling to tell me to start dinner. I'm not even going to answer it," and she headed to her parents' room.

However, the phone did not stop ringing, and finally in an irritated voice, she picked up the receiver and said, "Hello." She was shocked by the voice on the other end of the line.

"Hello," a girl's voice said. "I'm Amy. I was coming home from school, and I started thinking about you and how lonely you must be coming to a new school and not knowing anyone. For some reason, I just felt like I should give you a call and let you know that I care about you, and I am glad you are here. If you need anything or just need a friend to talk to, I'm here."

There was silence on the other end of the line as tears were streaming down the face of the girl who was just about to end her life. "Thank you," she cried. "You saved my life."

I remember the day when I heard that one of my friends had been rushed to the emergency room because she had been found cutting her wrists in desperation because she no longer wanted to live. I remember calling her the next day and hearing her voice on the line saying to me, "Jaclynn, I don't want to die. I thought life was not worth living anymore, and I didn't know what to do. I didn't realize until it was almost too late how much I don't want to die. I want to live."

She thought that her life was not very important and that she as a person was not very valuable. The only solution that she could come up with at the time was to end her life. In her mind, death was the perfect answer.

A teenage girl came to me during the Teen Spectacular after I had shared my experience of contemplating suicide at one point in my life and asked,

"Mrs. Weber, how do you stop yourself from wanting to commit suicide?"

I thought hers was a very interesting question. In other words, she was asking, "How do I make myself want to live? How do I learn that my life is important and that the decisions I make affect so many people—some who do not even exist yet?"

I am assuming that since someone had the courage to approach me with this question and since I had at one point during my teen years thought about suicide, there are many more who have thought about it or are thinking that to end it all would be a perfect answer.

Psalm 139:14 says, "*I will praise thee; for I am fearfully and wonderfully made....*"

Psalm 139:17 says, "*How precious also are thy thoughts unto me, O God!...*"

Matthew 10:31 says, "*...ye are of more value than many sparrows.*"

Genesis 1:27 says, "*So God created man in his own image, in the image of God created he him; male and female created he them.*"

The answer? I ran to the Bible. When you think that it is better for you to take your life by killing yourself, you are devaluing yourself down to nothing.

1. **If God created you, He must think you were worth creating.** If God thought enough of you to put you on the earth, then why are you questioning His judgment? Are you telling God He does not know what He is doing and that He made a mistake by putting you here?

2. **God does not make mistakes; people make mistakes.** If your parents were not married when you were conceived, you are not a mistake in God's eyes. God knew long before you were born that your parents were not going to be perfect and that you were going to be born into that family. He allowed it to happen because He wanted you to be born! He had a purpose for you in mind; He had people He wanted you to help. He had a person chosen for you to marry. He had a life for you to live that is worthwhile—all before you even existed. Are you a mistake? No! You are "...*fearfully and wonderfully made.*"

My Grandma Hyles wrote a book entitled *I Feel*

Precious to God. In her book she says that God sees you as a precious treasure; He values you more than any possession the world has to offer. He protects you, watches over you, and loves you more intimately than a groom loves his new bride. God thinks about you and loves you day after day, night after night. He says, "How precious also are My thoughts unto you." He never stops loving you.

3. **God chose you for a reason.** You are important to Him. No hatred from a friend, rejection by a boyfriend, abuse from a parent, or insult from an authority can change the fact that God loves you. Why would you just throw it all away because "He just doesn't love me anymore!" or "She won't even speak to me"?

When I was having a hard time, my dad used to say, "Just ride it out." The Bible says, "This too shall pass." If you can stick it out during the cloudy, stormy days, God has a beautiful rainbow waiting for you and a life that is worth living. Feel precious to God!

Afterword

THE CHRISTIAN LIFE IS not supposed to be a difficult, complicated, miserable path that finally ends in Heaven—if you make it. The life God planned for each one of us to live is supposed to be simple and happy, but there are some right choices that must be made.

The Bible says in Matthew 7:13, "...*for wide is the gate, and broad is the way, that leadeth to destruction....*" Sometimes it seems that the popular crowd chooses the wrong way, and it may not always be easy to choose the right way. When you are faced with decisions, remember that the wrong road **always** leads to destruction, and the right road **always** leads to happiness and contentment.

Doing right always pays off, and you will never regret taking "the road less traveled." At times you

may be lonely, but yours will be a life filled with joy, excitement, happiness, and peace.

The first step in taking the less-traveled road is knowing for sure that you are on your way to Heaven. If you were to die today, are you 100 percent sure that you would spend eternity in Heaven? You need to realize the following:

- **Realize there is none good.** Romans 3:10 says, "*As it is written, There is none righteous, no, not one.*"

- **See yourself as a sinner.** Romans 3:23 says, "*For all have sinned, and come short of the glory of God.*"

- **Recognize where sin came from.** Romans 5:12 says, "*Wherefore, as by one man sin entered into the world, and death by sin; and so death passed upon all men, for that all have sinned.*"

- **Notice God's price on sin.** Romans 6:23 says, "*For the wages of sin is death; but the gift of God is eternal life through Jesus Christ our Lord.*"

- **Realize that Christ died for you.** Romans 5:8 says, "*But God commendeth his love toward us, in that, while we were yet sinners, Christ died for us.*"

- **Take God at His Word.** Romans 10:13 says, "*For

whosoever shall call upon the name of the Lord shall be saved."

• **Claim God's promise for your salvation.** Romans 10:9-11 says, *"That if thou shalt confess with thy mouth the Lord Jesus, and shalt believe in thine heart that God hath raised him from the dead, thou shalt be saved. For with the heart man believeth unto righteousness; and with the mouth confession is made unto salvation. For the scripture saith, Whosoever believeth on him shall not be ashamed."*

Now pray. Confess that you are a sinner. Ask God to save you and receive Christ as your personal Saviour.

compiled by Jaclynn Weber

christianwomanhood.org